The Story of the
CAPITOL

By Marilyn Prolman

Illustrations by Bob O'Malley

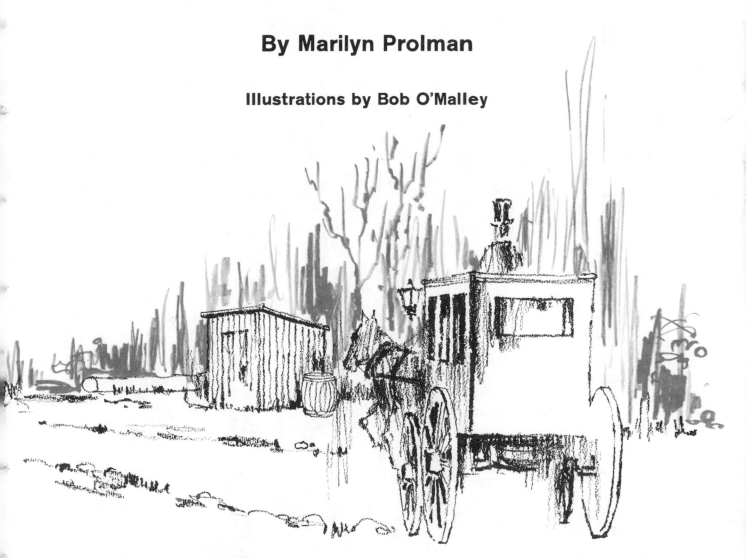

 CHILDRENS PRESS, CHICAGO

Library of Congress Catalog Card Number: 69-14681

4 5 6 7 8 9 10 11 12 13 14 15 16 17 18 19 20 21 22 23 24 25   R   75

"I see white buildings glistening in the sun. I see wide avenues and tree-lined parks. In the exact center of the city, on Jenkins Heights, I see the Capitol. This will be the home of the Congress, the men who make the laws for our new nation."

The man talking was Pierre L'Enfant, a city planner and engineer. It was a sunny day, and he and President George Washington were making a tour of the wooded, swampy land on the banks of the Potomac River. They had helped choose this site for the new capital city of the United States.

"It will be a beautiful city," said the President. The District of Columbia was a good choice. It is in the middle of our fourteen states, halfway between Massachusetts and Georgia."

"Yes, and there are many important cities nearby. The capital will be close enough to the ocean so people can get to it easily. I only wish I could live to see the city finished," said L'Enfant.

"Now that we have the land on Jenkins Heights for the Capitol," said Washington, "we must choose an architect to design the building for us."

"I can't think of an architect good enough to design such an important building. But I'm sure someone can do it. How shall we find him?" asked L'Enfant.

"Perhaps we could advertise in the newspapers," Washington suggested.

So it was that in 1792 an unusual advertisement appeared in newspapers throughout the United States of America. It announced a contest for designing the Capitol building. A prize of five hundred dollars was offered for the best design.

Closing day for the contest arrived. Many plans and designs had been submitted. Some were very beautiful and elaborate. Some were almost ridiculous, like the one with the oversize weathervane perched on its dome. Some were acceptable, but no plan seemed really suitable. The judges debated for a long time, but they reached no decision.

Three months after the contest ended, a young man named William Thornton asked if he could submit a design. "We have not yet made a decision," said one of the judges, "so it can do no harm. We will accept your design, but hurry. We cannot wait much longer."

When Thornton's design arrived, the judges knew it was what they had been waiting for. The drawing showed a classical building with two wings joined by a dome at the center.

"Grandeur, simplicity, and convenience appear to be well combined in this plan," said George Washington in his official comment on the design. The judges awarded the prize to Thornton and appointed him Architect of the Capitol.

"Who is this William Thornton, and why have I never heard of him?" Pierre L'Enfant asked President Washington.

"Until now he has been known as Dr. William Thornton," said Washington. "He is a physician by training. He has also been a portrait painter and a steamboat experimenter. When he read of our contest, he decided to become an architect and taught himself from books. He is a brilliant man."

"And he has given us an inspired design," added L'Enfant.

The laying of the cornerstone for the Capitol took place in 1793. It was a day of great celebration in Washington, D.C. All the residents of the village paraded to Jenkins Heights. Many government officials came to see President Washington lay the cornerstone. After the solemn ceremony, the real festivities began. A five-hundred pound ox was barbecued and served to the guests. There were dancing, singing, shouting, and general merriment. A display of fireworks ended the evening celebration.

The building of the first wing of the Capitol was soon under way, but it did not go very smoothly. Many problems slowed down the work. The Building Commissioners were not happy with the progress. They called William Thornton to appear before them.

"Why is the building going so slowly?" they asked.

"There are many reasons. First, there is not

enough money. You promised to sell land in the village to pay for the building," Thorton said.

"The lots haven't sold quite so well as we expected. But until they do, we will borrow money for your building," answered the Commissioners.

"Money will help somewhat, but there are other problems. We need a large number of tools, and it isn't always possible to find enough. Without the proper tools, the work cannot be done.

"Also, materials arrive late. The roads leading to the city are bad. Transportation is slow. And the rain we have had lately does not help," Thornton added.

"These are problems you must solve," said the Commissioners. "We don't mean to be harsh with you."

"There is one other problem, gentlemen," said Thornton. "Stephen Hallet, my assistant, won second prize in the contest. He thinks he can use his ideas instead of mine. He defies me at every turn. I cannot work with the man."

"If it will keep the peace and speed construction of the building, we will dismiss him," said the Commissioners. "Is there anything else?"

"No," said Thornton. "Everything should be fine now."

Thornton worked hard. In spite of all his problems, the north wing of the building was completed in the autumn of 1800. But one wing was not big enough.

With the 32-man Senate, the 106-man House of Representatives, the Supreme Court, the Circuit Court, and the Library of Congress all using the same building, it was tremendously overcrowded.

When the first session of Congress was held there, President John Adams made a speech praising the building. "I congratulate the people of the United States on the assembly of Congress at the permanent seat of their government, and I congratulate you, gentlemen, on the prospect of a residence not to be changed," he said.

The seat of the government did not change, but the residence did. It was difficult for everyone to work in the crowded building. In 1801 the House of Representatives moved to a temporary, one-story home built on the site of the present south wing. This oval-shaped structure proved to be even more temporary than planned. When the members of the House gathered together, the heat in the building was unbearable. It soon earned the nickname, the "Oven." After three years the representatives could not stand the heat any longer. They gave up and moved back to the overcrowded north wing.

In 1804 the "Oven" was knocked down and construction on the south wing began. William Thornton was now head of the Patent Office. Benjamin Henry Latrobe was selected to replace Thornton as the architect.

Latrobe supervised the construction of the south wing, which matched the north wing. He designed a magnificent chamber for the House of Representatives. The finished room had classical columns with corn and tobacco decorations. A visitor's gallery was also included. President Thomas Jefferson, an amateur architect himself, praised it.

However, Representative John Randolph of Virginia did not. "The room is handsome and fit for anything but the use intended," he said. "The echoes make it difficult to hear people speak. And, from many spots in this chamber you can hear a whisper from across the room, but you cannot hear a whisper from the man sitting next to you."

The chamber proved to be a difficult place in which to work. The echoes made it almost impossible to carry on business. House members hung red woolen draperies in the hope that they could muffle some of the sound.

Meanwhile, the walls in the old Senate chamber in the north wing had begun to crack. The ceiling leaked whenever it rained. Latrobe remodeled the wing, and made it into a two-story building. The Supreme Court moved into the small first floor, and the Senate moved upstairs.

Now the two wings of the Capitol were completed. A wooden walkway connected the two sections. The building on Jenkins Heights was beginning to take shape.

Meanwhile, England had been attacking American ships on the ocean. Some Americans talked of the possibility of war. Inside the Capitol building angry debates went on between the "War Hawks," and those in favor of peace. Among the most outspoken War Hawks were Henry Clay and John C. Calhoun. "We must declare war against Great Britain," cried Calhoun. "She does not treat us like an independent nation. We are not involved in her war with France."

"England has committed the worst crime of all," added Clay. "She has taken American sailors off American ships and forced them to serve in the British navy!"

Congress was soon won over to the side of the War Hawks. On June 18, the United States declared war on Great Britain. The War of 1812 began. For two years most of the fighting took place far away from the Capitol building. But in the summer of 1814 Rear Admiral Sir George Cockburn landed his British squadron in Maryland. They captured Washington on August 24 and began to set fire to most of the government buildings.

Late at night Admiral Cockburn led his men into the House chamber. "Shall we burn this building, men?" he asked.

"Aye!" they shouted in reply.

"Then gather all the books, desks, and chairs into

the middle of the room and set them ablaze!" When this was done he cried, "On to the next room!"

It rained later that night. Only the rain saved the city from total destruction. The next day, a powerful windstorm swept through the city. Buildings toppled, trees fell. Thirty British soldiers were killed. These events and the threat of an American attack frightened the British out of the city.

When Latrobe inspected the Capitol, he remarked, "The devastation is dreadful. The building is a most magnificent ruin." The interiors of the House and Senate chambers were completely burned out, and their exteriors blackened. The wooden walkway joining the two buildings was destroyed. Latrobe bravely began the job of rebuilding.

Congress found a temporary home in a building across the street. It became known as the "Brick Capitol." The House and Senate stayed there while Latrobe repaired the burned-out Capitol. Congressional business was carried on as usual inside the brick building. Part of that business included the ratification of the Treaty of Ghent which ended the War of 1812.

16

Meanwhile, Latrobe strengthened both wings of the Capitol. He replaced the burned wood with sandstone and marble, brick and steel. He enlarged the Senate chamber and redesigned the inside of the House chamber to lessen the echoes. But Latrobe, like William Thornton, also had problems. After several disagreements with the Building Commissioners, he resigned in 1817.

Charles Bulfinch of Boston replaced Latrobe. Bulfinch was the first American-born architect appointed to work on the Capitol. Following the original designs of Thorton and Latrobe, he supervised the building of the central section and the Rotunda, a large circular hall covered by a dome. The cornerstone for the center section was laid in 1818. By 1824, construction on the Rotunda was almost completed, and the large circular hall was used to welcome the famous Revolutionary War hero, the Marquis de Lafayette.

By 1850 the Capitol was once again overcrowded. The nation had expanded westward. New states had been admitted to the Union. The number of senators had reached 62 and the representatives, 232. "We must have more space," said many of the congressmen. The drive for more space was led by Jefferson Davis, the man who would one day leave the United States Senate to become President of the Confederate States of America.

The expansion of the Capitol was begun. Thomas V. Walter was selected by President Millard Fillmore as the new architect. Walter designed new buildings to be added to the north and south wings. The old Senate and House chambers were abandoned. The old buildings would serve as connections between the new additions and the central Rotunda.

Walter remained Architect of the Capitol for fifteen years. During that time he tripled the size of the building. He built new legislative halls with paneled walls and glass and iron skylights. His design made it easier for the congressmen to hear what was said in the chambers. He installed gas lighting which was very modern at that time. To enhance the elegance of the hall, Walter replaced the desks in the House chamber with settees. But the members found that their business was serious enough to require desks, and the desks were returned.

The late 1850's were dangerous years in the Capitol. Long debates on slavery took place. The southern states wanted to continue the practice; the northern states did not. Threats of withdrawing from the Union were heard, as were threats of violence.

"Every man on the floor of both houses is armed with a revolver," said Senator James H. Hammond of South Carolina. "One man dropped his weapon during a tense moment, and I thought that the entire Senate would turn into a violent mob."

In 1861 the southern states withdrew from the Union. Senator Jefferson Davis of Mississippi stood on the Senate floor and said, "I go hence, not in hostility to you, but in love and allegiance to her [Mississippi]." Davis left the Senate and was followed by senators and representatives from South Carolina, Florida, Alabama, Georgia, Louisiana, and Texas.

When President Abraham Lincoln took the oath of office on the Capitol steps, the Union was divided. In his inauguration speech Lincoln said, "I consider that the Union is unbroken.

"In your hands, my dissatisfied fellow-countrymen, and not in mine, is the momentous issue of civil war. The government will not assail you. You can have no conflict without being yourselves the aggressors.

"We are not enemies, but friends. We must not be enemies."

A little more than a month later, the Civil War began. Congress was not meeting when the fighting broke out. The War Department took over the Capitol building and used it as a barracks for the Union troops. The men who were stationed there called it the "Big Tent."

At one time, three thousand soldiers slept in the building. The first men to arrive were quartered in the legislative chambers, where each man had a desk. At night the men slept under the desks. When all the desks were taken, the men overflowed into the halls. In the Rotunda the soldiers slept under the unfinished dome.

Furnaces in the basement were used for cooking rations of biscuits, bacon, and coffee. Eventually the basement was turned into a bakery. The walls of small storage rooms were bricked up and made into huge ovens. Enough bread was baked here to feed the soldiers in all the forts around Washington.

By autumn, however, the Capitol served another purpose. It was equipped with cots and served as an emergency hospital. Victims of the battles of Antietam and Second Manassas were treated there. When all the patients had been transferred to other hospitals, Congress returned to its quarters.

Throughout the war construction continued on the Capitol. President Lincoln said, "If the people see

construction on the Capitol go on, it will be a sign that we intend the Union shall go on." Architect Thomas Walter's task now was to finish the big dome that he had designed for the central Rotunda. The dome he built, which tops the Capitol today, was hailed as a masterpiece of engineering skill.

The dome has inner and outer cast iron shells which are intricately bolted together. Between the two shells is a narrow staircase of 183 steps. To lift the heavy iron parts of the dome into place, a towering scaffold was built. The scaffold went up through the dome from the floor of the Rotunda. Hoisting devices were mounted on the scaffold and heavy materials could be lifted to the dome from outside the building.

When the dome was finished, a statue was placed at the top. This bronze sculpture was done by an American artist, Thomas Crawford. He called it "Armed Liberty." The statue is of a woman 19 feet, 6 inches tall. She wears a classical robe, and holds a sword in her right hand and a wreath resting on a shield in her left. The statue was made in five sections. Each had to be hoisted to the top of the dome separately and fastened into place. At a special ceremony in 1863 the last piece of "Armed Liberty," the head, was raised and bolted into place.

The next task was the building of the columned porticoes and pediments around all the entrances.

It was not until 1916 that the sculptured east pediment of the House was finished.

The Capitol today still is not completed. Work on the building goes on all the time. In 1955 another major addition was finished, and in 1961 its old sandstone front was replaced by marble.

The present Architect of the Capitol is J. George Stewart, who was appointed by President Dwight Eisenhower.

"I am busy all the time," says Stewart. "I have considered plans for a four-level, 2000-car garage under the Capitol Plaza. It has even been suggested that I build an outdoor restaurant. Part of my job is to pick and choose among the thousands of suggestons that come into my office every year."

The Capitol complex today is almost a city in itself. The building now serves 100 senators and 435 representatives. It has post offices, ticket offices, telegraph offices, and stationery stores. One can eat at snack bars, cafeterias, and restaurants. The Capitol has its own libraries, purchasing offices, even warehouses. Senators and representatives can get free haircuts in congressional barber shops. Congresswomen can find beauty shops without leaving the Capitol complex.

A special, small subway, with cars that seat twelve people, makes regular runs from the Senate and House office buildings to the Capitol. Senators, representatives, and the more than seven thousand men

and women who work for them find the subway system indispensable.

The Capitol has its own police force of 216 men appointed by the members of Congress. Many of these police are students interested in government. Congress also has its own medical officer and two staff physicians to take care of its members.

A Prayer Room is open to congressmen of all faiths during all legislative sessions. Over its altar is a stained-glass window which shows George Washington kneeling in prayer.

Great works of art are everywhere in the Capitol building. The Rotunda is the center of the building and the center of the Capitol's art collection. The eight large oil paintings that hang in the Rotunda show scenes of the discovery and colonization of the country.

The old, echoing House chamber of the early nineteenth century now serves as Statuary Hall. When it was set aside for this purpose, each state was asked to send two bronze or marble statues to be displayed. Statues of distinguished citizens were sent from all over the country. There were statues of pioneers, soldiers, statesmen, inventors. So many statues arrived that it was feared that the floor would not be able to support their weight. Now only one statue from each state stands in the hall; the others are elsewhere in the building.

Statues of the favorite sons and daughters from all the fifty states are represented in the collection in Statuary Hall. Henry Clay, John C. Calhoun, and Daniel Webster call to mind the great debates that took place on the floor of the Senate over slavery and preservation of the Union. Ethan Allen, one of Vermont's Green Mountain Boys, brings back the memory of the Revolution. Father Jacques Marquette and Brigham Young were important figures in westward

expansion. Will Rogers, a favorite son of Oklahoma, is also represented. Rogers once called Congress the "Washington joke factory."

Under the dome of the central Rotunda, seventeen men have been honored with State funerals. Four of them were Presidents: Abraham Lincoln, James Garfield, William McKinley, and John F. Kennedy. Others included such men as the Unknown Soldiers of World War I, World War II, and the Korean War. In 1909, Pierre L'Enfant, the man who had chosen the spot on which the Capitol stands, was given a belated tribute here.

Presidents of the United States begin their terms of office by taking the Presidential oath at the Capitol. Thomas Jefferson was the first. In 1829 the ceremony was moved outdoors by Andrew Jackson. He wanted to give the crowd a better view of history in the making. Since then many other Presidents have been inaugurated on the east front porch of the building.

American history is everywhere in the nation's Capitol. It is seen in the paintings, frescoes, and sculptures throughout the building. The walls echo with the voices of history, the halls resound with them. History has been made here, is being made here, and will be made here. The Capitol is an ever-growing building in an ever-growing nation, the United States of America.